So you THINK you want to get married?

By SKIP and BEVERLY LITTLE

xulon PRESS

Copyright © 2016 by Skip and Beverly Little

So you THINK you want to get married?
by Skip and Beverly Little

Printed in the United States of America.

Edited by Xulon Press.

ISBN 9781498459914

All rights reserved solely by the author. The author guarantees all contents are original and do not infringe upon the legal rights of any other person or work. No part of this book may be reproduced in any form without the permission of the author. The views expressed in this book are not necessarily those of the publisher.

Unless otherwise indicated, Scripture quotations taken from the New King James Version (NKJV). Copyright © 1982 by Thomas Nelson, Inc. Used by permission. All rights reserved.

www.xulonpress.com

Table of Contents

Introduction		vii
Chapter I:	So What Do You Think God Says?	11
Chapter II:	So What Do You Think about God's Timing?	17
Chapter III:	So What Do You Think is Behind the Mask?	23
Chapter IV:	So What Should You "Be"come Before Marriage?	45
Chapter V:	So What Should You Think about Sex?	65
Chapter VI:	So What Should You Think about Roles in Marriage?	83
Chapter VII:	So What Should You Expect?	101
Chapter VIII:	So What Should You Think about Parental Guidance?	111

Introduction

Many people get married expecting to stay in it for a lifetime. Unfortunately, the constant increase in the divorce rate has proven that in today's society, this is not the case. There are a number of factors that have led to this increase, such as; relying on feelings and emotions rather than facts, not being educated on what is required in marriage, and being rushed into marriage because of age or peer pressure.

The principles from *So You Think You Want to Get Married* will inspire you to consider a new way of approaching marriage. Through each chapter, you will gain valuable insight that will equip you to make informed decisions about yourself and your potential spouse *before* you are joined in marriage.

As you begin the first chapter, *So What Do You Think God Says*, you will be guided through what it means to hear God's voice and understand the direction and timing He is giving you every step of the way. Who could go wrong with gaining direction from the God of the universe? By truly embracing the principles set forth in **So You Think You Want to Get Married**, you will be enlightened about the person God has designed to be your life mate.

Several months ago a young lady shared the value of the principles from this book. She was in a committed long term relationship with her boyfriend. But once she applied the principles from, *So What Do You Think God Says?*, she began to realize that her longtime boyfriend was not the life mate God intended for her. A few months later, after walking away from the relationship and continuing to study these principles, she was led to the person God had for her. She is now happily married with four beautiful children.

Take each chapter and thoroughly unpack it so you can identify areas you and your potential spouse need to consider before getting married. If you do the work required and address any unsettling issues, you will move from "So you think…" to "So you know…" Or, you may discover that you want to wait or even remain single!!!"

How do I Embrace Adopting a Healthy Mindset about Marriage?

Once you begin to discern God's voice and His timing by applying the principles in the first two chapters, God will begin to show you the "true" you and help you identify truths about your potential spouse. Areas of concern will become evident in Chapter III: *So What Do You Think is Behind the Mask?* and *Chapter IV: So What Should You Think About "Be"coming Before Marriage?* Remember, the goal is to move from thinking to knowing, so just seek God and discern His voice as you go through the exercises in this book. Remember, now is not the time to put on blinders but to allow the truth to be revealed before you make the life altering commitment to marry.

Prior to our marriage, I learned Skip had a disconnected relationship with his Dad. It had gone on for twenty years. Once I began to peel back the mask, I discovered my potential spouse (at the time) had a problem with forgiveness. That was a huge problem for me. If he did not have the ability to somehow forgive his father, I was concerned that I may do something that would be unforgivable. Forgiveness is a critical component of marriage so this issue had to be resolved.

What's The Big Barrier?

In this day and age maintaining a "dating" relationship while remaining sexually pure is extremely rare. The reality is that those who do not remain sexually pure find themselves in drama-filled relationships that inhibit their ability to make sound decisions about marriage. In many cases, pre-marital sex will cloud your view and skew what is really going on between you and your potential spouse. In *Chapter V: So What Should You Think about Sex,* you will learn that sexual impurity before marriage may result in one or both people engaging in activities that can cause serious damage during the marriage. When a woman's purity is protected before marriage, she feels honored and her future husband receives the respect that God intended for him.

There are a number of people who have based their decision to Marry on "good sex," only to discover that there are so many other components to marriage.

What Will Marriage Require of Me?

Two of the most important chapters in this book are: *So What Should You Think about Roles in Marriage* and *So What Should You Expect?* These chapters will guide you through the specific roles of a husband and a wife and will also discuss spousal expectations. You will gain a solid understanding of what will be expected of you as a husband or wife and what you will need to do to meet those expectations. Day-to-day life steps in to marriage right after the honeymoon and it changes the landscape of your marital expectations. Most couples are not prepared for this. These chapters will help you honestly assess whether or not you are equipped to handle these roles and expectations.

Many troubled marriages begin with false expectations and a misunderstanding of marital roles. These chapters will help you avoid such conflicts. Imagine being on a job without clearly defined roles and responsibilities. You would constantly show poor performance, which is what happens in marriage.

Once you complete this section, the question of whether to marry or wait should be clearer to you. For those of you who are without a potential spouse, take your time going through the chapters and complete the exercises that apply. You will be ahead of the game when your potential spouse comes along.

Chapter VIII: *So What Should You Think about Parental Guidance?* This chapter highlights the lost appreciation for the wisdom that comes from parents or authority figures in your life. We will address what it means to have parental guidance before marriage. Here we ask that you empower your parents or those in authority over you to pose the questions they feel they no longer have a right to ask. Allow them to offer their own wisdom, personal advice and invaluable gifts to you during your decision making process.

When you choose to marry, not only are you marrying the person you love so dearly but you will also enter a lifelong relationship with that person's family. Therefore having parental guidance and approval of your marriage is needed to significantly reduce many family challenges that can occur.

Marriage alone can have its challenges. It's best to get everyone's approval and gain harmony from the beginning. Parental Guidance is advised!

Now let's move from "thinking" to "knowing!"

Chapter I:

So What Do You Think God Says?

Hearing the Voice of God

Hearing God's voice is directly related to knowing His will for your life. One bad decision, one wrong move can have major ramifications for your life. When you are exactly where God wants you to be, there is no safer place. The decisions that life brings require keen discernment and the knowledge that it is God who has spoken.

John 10:27 says, the sheep of God know the voice of God. Those of us who follow God are His sheep. We know how to recognize and follow His voice. This is key because every voice that you hear is not God's voice. Many reject the voice of God because they do not agree with what they hear or they do not understand it. But God never asks us to understand. He asks us to trust Him and obey.

> God never asks us to understand. He asks us to trust Him and obey.

God speaks to His people in several different ways:

THE WORD:

The primary way that God speaks is through His Word which are the 66 books of the Bible. When you feel that God is speaking, what you have heard must agree with His Word. He will never tell you to do something that is contrary to His Word. If it is contrary, it is not God who is speaking.

Hebrews 4:12NIV tells us *"the Word of God is living and active. Sharper than any double edged sword, it penetrates even to dividing soul and spirit, joints and marrow; it judges the thoughts and attitude of the heart."* God's Word is living and powerful. It is precise and specific enough to speak directly to your life and situation. Psalm 119:105 reminds us that the Word that God has given us will illuminate what choice to make and which path to take. It will help us to see clearly when we are unsure about which way to go or where to turn.

PRAYER & INNER CONVICTION:

God also speaks during your prayer time. Prayer means communication. It is not just you talking to God. It requires that you listen to Him as well. Once you pray, you must give God time to speak.

He also gives us inner convictions. Romans 8:16NIV reminds us that the Spirit Himself testifies with our spirit that we are God's children. There is a shaking of hands between God's spirit and your spirit. He will give you an inner release or thought that will settle you. Learn to sit quietly and allow Him to bring an agreement between His spirit and yours. Acts 22:19-21 provides an example of this principle through the life of Paul.

AUTHORITY & GODLY COUNSEL:

God gives direction and speaks through the authorities that He has placed in your life. Repeatedly, He tells us that we are to submit to the authorities in our lives. Proverbs 21:1NIV says, *"The King's heart is in the hands of the Lord, he directs it like the watercourse wherever He pleases."* God has the ability to control the heart of the authorities in your life. Therefore, you should not try to manipulate the heart of those in authority over you. It is not your job to discern how that person is being led. As long as they are not leading you to do something ungodly or unbiblical, you should follow their guidance. When you disobey authority, you are in essence, disobeying God.

Sometimes you are called to honor and other times you are called to obey. There's a difference between the two. Ephesians 6:1 says, children are called to obey their parents. In this instance, you simply do what you are told. To honor authority is to give great weight to their counsel although you are not required to submit to it. It is a point of influence in your life. To obey authority requires you to do what they say to do. Family, government, employment, and church are the four primary sources of authority.

Not all counsel is godly. You must make sure that you are receiving counsel from those who are godly. Proverbs 11:14 says, *"Where there is no counsel, the people perish but in the multitude of counselors there is safety."* God can use this as a means of clear direction (see also Proverbs 24:6).

> Not all counsel is godly. You must make sure that you are receiving counsel from those who are godly. Proverbs 11:14 says, "Where there is no counsel, the people perish but in the multitude of counselors there is safety."

So You THINK You Want To Get Married

SITUATIONS & CIRCUMSTANCES:

God orders your steps and orchestrates the circumstances in your life. Where there is a vision, there is also provision. Trying to orchestrate events with your own power is not the will of God.

Many make the mistake of wanting the thing that God prohibits. He closes one door and directs you to another but that is not the door that you want to go through. So, you try to work to make things happen to support your desires. In this case, you go against the situation that is presented and against what God is trying to do in your life. You must be sensitive to the opening and closing of doors in your life.

In Philippians 4:19 you are told that God will give you what you need in order to do what you need to do. If you don't have the resources, it may be a sign that it is not what God wants you to do.

In Genesis 22:13, God provides a sacrifice for Abraham when it looked as if he would have to sacrifice his only son. God confirmed what Abraham was to do through the situation. He miraculously provided a ram caught in the bushes.

FLEECES:

A fleece is when you ask God to give you an indication of His will by showing you a specific sign. In Judges 6:36-39, Gideon puts out a fleece and asks God to do a specific act as an indication that He had, in fact, spoken. It is important to note that eventually you will have to graduate from relying on the spectacular in order to hear from God. This is because it is easy for the devil to interfere when you use fleeces. As your relationship grows, you can hear God's voice clearly and you will no longer need a fleece (see also Genesis 24).

Fleeces must be progressive and not preventive. You must be willing to say to God, "I will not move forward until you speak to me." Your posture must not be, "I'm moving forward unless you stop me."

> You must be willing to say to God, "I will not move forward until you speak to me."

DREAMS & VISIONS:

There are numerous passages of scripture that attest to God speaking to people through dreams or visions. Not all dreams come from God. Some of your dreams are a reflection of your inner desires, passions and lust. Therefore you must be sure your dreams are God inspired.

This section is not intended to be exhaustive. It is biblically based and represents ways that we have personally experienced hearing God's voice in our life. For a more comprehensive study, the complete 4-CD series entitled, Hearing the Voice of God, can be obtained from the online Media Center of The First Baptist Church of Glenarden at www.fbcglenarden.org.

Pastor John K. Jenkins, Sr.
First Baptist Church of Glenarden

Chapter II:

So What Do You Think about God's Timing?
(Taken from the teachings of Pastor John K. Jenkins, Sr.)

Hearing God's voice in regards to your potential spouse is only one half of the equation. It is equally important to consider God's timing. Getting married at the wrong time can be just as bad as marrying the wrong person. Unfortunately, we struggle with knowing God's timing because we do not know the plans the Lord has for our lives. Jeremiah 8:7 tells us the animals know their season. However, due to deceit and rebellion we, as humans, often miss God's timing.

Ecclesiastes 3:1-11:17 tells us that everything has an appropriate time. This is God's plan. However, Satan's plan is to move us away from God's timeframe. Many times he attempts to expose us to things prematurely so we will not receive God's full blessings. For example, the prodigal son was exposed to his inheritance prematurely and ended up mishandling the blessings God had for him. The inheritance was his, but he failed to wait on God's timing to receive it.

> Getting married at the wrong time can be just as bad as marrying the wrong person.

Read Luke 15:11-16. What is God saying to you in this passage?

Things you should know about God's Timing:

> We may think something should happen in a year, but God's plan may be for it to happen in two years.

1. **Realize that God's view of time is different than man's view.**

   II Peter 3:8NIV says, "Be not ignorant of this one thing, with the Lord a day is like a thousand years and a thousand years is like a day."

   We may think something should happen in a year, but God's plan may be for it to happen in two years. Sometimes our parents or godly authority may tell us we need to wait before getting married, which, in most cases, is God speaking through them and telling us it is not our season for marriage. The ultimate goal is to be in tune with God's timing so you can be in His perfect will.

   The right time always brings glory to God. In John 12:23-27, Jesus predicts His death. This passage shows us how Jesus operated in God's timing. Even though Jesus was troubled, His ultimate goal was to glorify God. Is your ultimate goal to glorify God, or is it all about you?

2. **Properly observe and understand events as a basis for figuring out God's timing.** *In Luke 12:54-56NIV, Jesus said to the crowd "when you see a cloud rising in the west, immediately you say It's going to rain and it does. And when the south wind blows, you say It's going to be hot and it is. Hypocrites! You know how to interpret the appearance of the earth and the sky, how is it that you don't know how to interpret this present time?"*

   Just as we know when it will rain or snow, God wants us to observe and know the timing of events in our own lives. To do that you must study God's Word and His plan for marriage regularly and evaluate if the desires of your flesh out weigh your desire to fulfill God's will in our life.

   Answer this question: Will the decision to get married bring glory to God?

3. **If the desires of your flesh are greater than God's will for your life, you become more willing to violate Biblical principles to get married.**

Ask yourself the following questions:

- **Is your potential spouse still married? If so, Mark 10:9 tells us "What God has joined together, let no man separate."**

- **Do your parents or those in authority over you disapprove of your relationship? If so, Ephesians 6:1 teaches us to honor our parents (see details on honoring parents in Chapter 8).**

- **Are you considering marrying an unbeliever? If so, II Corinthians 6:14 teaches us to avoid being unequally yoked with unbelievers. This means we should not marry someone who does not have the same Christian values and beliefs.**

- Have you put your potential spouse before the things of God? If so, you have violated what God teaches us. Exodus 20:3 says we should not place anything before God.

- Are you anxious to get married? If so, Philippians 4:6 teaches, "be anxious for nothing, but in prayer and supplication make your request known to God."

- In addition to the ways listed above, list some other ways you could be violating biblical principles.

- **Summarize what you believe God is saying to you about His timing for marriage.**

Chapter III:

So What Do You Think is Behind the Mask?

Huffington Post reported that a survey showed that most people select a spouse based on external attributes. The problem with this is a person can use their external qualities to hide who they really are in order to appease another person. Qualities that are attractive in dating relationships are not the same qualities that will sustain a marriage. A person's external attributes should not be a deciding factor when selecting a spouse. What should be considered is a person's character and values.

In many dating relationships, people tend to mask who they really are. Some do so intentionally, while others do it unintentionally. A mask is a cover for the face used to disguise a person's true identity. It conceals one's genuine character or intentions.

In relationships, "wearing masks" causes people to marry individuals they do not really know. It is natural for people to put their "best face forward," however, marriage-seekers must remember that masks crack and over time the real person will slowly be revealed. Therefore, it is best to remove the mask ***before*** you say "I do."

> Qualities that are attractive in dating relationships are not the same qualities that will sustain a marriage.

Taking off your mask to uncover your true self is not easy. It requires a great deal of self-examination, honesty, and prayer from both parties in the relationship. If you realize that you are wearing a mask, ask God for the courage to be vulnerable. If you are uncovering your potential spouse's mask, ask God for wisdom to look beyond the outward appearance. Revealing your true self and looking for the true identity of your potential spouse helps to strengthen the foundation as the relationship progresses.

I Samuel 16:7 says, *"For the Lord does not see as man sees, for man looks at the outward appearance, but the Lord looks at the heart."* In this passage, the Lord is telling us to look beyond what we see on the outside.

Meditate on this passage and evaluate how you view yourself and/or your potential spouse. Are you primarily captivated by how they look? Are you lured by material possessions or status? If you answered yes to one or both of these questions you should examine whether you can sustain this relationship once the mask is removed. Remember, what is revealed as you remove the mask will play a significant role in your future marriage.

Mike and Josephine

Mike and Josephine were in a two-year courting relationship. They were committed to celibacy until marriage, however, Mike did not reveal that he was a nymphomaniac. Mike spent countless hours indulging in social networking. He connected with various women to engage in sexual encounters. Josephine was aware of the long hours Mike spent social networking online. Deep inside, she had concerns, but she suppressed them and married Mike anyway.

- **What do you think will happen in their marriage?**

- **What could Josephine have done prior to marriage?**

- **What causes us to suppress our concerns?**

- **How would you handle this situation?**

There are certain areas in your potential spouse's life that you should examine closely. As you look at each of these areas, be honest with yourself. Remember that what you see in a person is typically what you get. Do not seek to camouflage obvious issues by making excuses for the person. Remember that you have the freedom to walk away. More importantly, remember that you cannot change a person. Only God can!

Reveal

Before you make a marital commitment, you must do your best to determine who your potential spouse really is. Engage in conversations that will bring hidden truths to light. You must ask questions and listen carefully to the responses that you receive. This is the only way that you will discover whether your potential spouse is hiding their real identity. When you are asked hard questions, answer them as honestly as you can.

If you are the person hiding behind the mask, it is time to reveal your true self. Do not be reluctant or fearful that you are in a "last chance" scenario. God wants what is true and best for you and your potential spouse. You must want the same.

Psalm 139:14 says, *"We are fearfully and wonderfully made…."* Because many people do not believe this about themselves due to past hurts and failures, some are driven to hide their true identity. Do you believe you are fearfully and wonderfully made? Can you be free to be who God created you to be? If not, what is keeping you from believing what God believes about you? Share your insight with your potential spouse or an accountability partner.

Consider the following:

- What are some things people do to mask who they really are?

- What things have you done to mask the real you?

- Why do you think you are masking who you really are?

Relationships

It is important to examine the health of your potential spouse's relationships with their parents, siblings, friends, co-workers and authority figures.

In Ephesians 5 and 6 Paul says to submit to one another and to honor your parents. If your potential spouse is disrespectful to a parent, then chances are they will be disrespectful to you. If she is not submissive to her boss, she likely will not be submissive

God created us as relational beings. Therefore it is important that we are interacting with each other in a healthy manner.

to you. If he changes friends every year, this may indicate that there is a pattern of disloyalty or lack of commitment in relationships and is clearly a sign that he will not be committed to you.

Examine the Health of your Relationship:

- **Describe your own relationships with your parents, your children (if applicable), your boss, and your friends.**

- **Describe your potential spouse's relationships with his/her parents, children (if applicable), boss and friends.**

- **How would you describe your relationship with God?**

- Are there broken relationships or hurts that you are unwilling to forgive and reconcile? If so, describe them. Why is it so difficult for you to resolve?

- How might your broken and hurt relationships impact your future marriage?

Consider the following:

My husband had a twenty-year broken relationship with his father. This was troubling to me. If he was unable to forgive his father who had been with him since birth, what assurance did I have that I would be forgiven if I offended him? In order for me to agree to marry him, I needed to know that my future husband had the capacity to forgive. I was not able to convince him just how important forgiving his father was but the godly male authorities in his life did. They shared Scriptures with him and challenged him to be the Christian man God had called him to be. A few weeks later, he repented before God and began the reconciliation process with his Dad.

Proverbs 23:22 says to listen to your father that gave you life and do not despise your mother when she is old.

I Peter 5:5 teaches us to be submitted to those who are older.

Ephesians 6:2 tells us to honor our mothers and fathers.

Based on these passages answer the follow questions:

- **What is God saying about the importance of respect and submission in your life?**

- **How do you and your potential spouse exemplify respect and submission with authorities and in key relationships?**

Additional questions for divorcees only:

- **How did you contribute to the breakup of your previous marriage (if you do not think you contributed, that is a red flag)?**

- **What will you do differently this time?**

- **Are you willing to reconcile with your previous spouse? If not, why? Have you clearly heard the voice of God concerning which path you should take (Chapter1)?**

For additional guidance, read <u>Divorce and Remarriage</u>, by Tony Evans.

Finances

Financial disagreements are one of the major causes of divorce. Therefore, it is imperative that you examine your potential

> Financial disagreements are one of the major causes of divorce. Therefore, it is imperative that you examine your potential spouse's financial status prior to marriage.

So You THINK You Want To Get Married

Matthew 6:21 – Where we invest most is where our heart is.

spouse's financial status prior to marriage. Matthew 6:21 states, *"where your treasure is, there your heart will be also."* In this passage, God is telling us our hearts are driven towards what we treasure most.

George and Susie

George and Susie were in a three-year relationship and were planning to be married. Susie was an excessive spender with a poor credit score. George was aware of Susie's spending habits. He was not aware however, of just how far she was willing to go to satisfy her urges. In fact, Susie had been criminally prosecuted for writing bad checks. George could not believe that he had come so close to getting married without taking a closer look at the implications of Susie's extreme spending habits.

Assess you and your potential spouse's financial situation using the following questions:

- **Are they a saver or a spender?**

- **Does your potential spouse constantly buy items they really can't afford?**

- Does your potential spouse ask you for money to pay bills and other expenses?

- What is your credit score? What is your potential spouse's credit score? If his/her credit score is low, what are the causes (obtain credit reports and scores at creditkarma.com)? Do they have an honest plan to improve their credit?

  Note: when sharing scores and reports, please be mindful of identity theft.

Read Matthew 6:19-21 – which essentially teaches us where we invest is where our heart is and answer the remaining questions below.

- Do you and your potential spouse use the principle expressed in this passage to guide your purchasing decisions?

- Where does your potential spouse spend most of his/her money?

- How do you think a marriage can be affected by poor financial management?

Background Check

Oftentimes, businesses conduct a background check on potential employees. They know that a person's history and previous practices can predict the type of employee the candidate will likely be. Therefore, employers often check references, credit history, substance abuse history, and criminal history. The marital relationship is much more important, but unfortunately many people enter into marriage with no idea of their potential spouse's history.

II Timothy 3:1-9 essentially tells us that people will be lovers of themselves. They will have a form of godliness but really will not embrace the ways of God. Read the passage in its entirety.

- **Does this passage reflect you or your potential spouse in any way? If so, how?**

- **What do people say about your potential spouse? What is his/her reputation?**

Do as much research as possible to determine the type of person to whom you are about to commit.

- **What character qualities (i.e. integrity, dedication) would you say he/she possesses?**

Never enter into a covenant relationship with anyone who is abusive! God has something better in store for you!

If you do not know your potential spouse's reputation, ask people who may know him/her so you can find out the truth. Close family members, for example are often willing to share information. If the person has been divorced, review the divorce decree. Ask what caused the divorce and what role your potential spouse played in it. If he/she does not take any responsibility for the divorce, that is a huge issue and is very concerning.

It is often said that birds of a feather flock together. A person's friends are an indication of who they are – good or bad. If you see things in your potential spouse's friends that you do not like, discuss them. Do not accept excuses. Do as much research as possible. It is important to determine the type of person you are about to commit to. Be open to receiving information and feedback from people who have known your potential spouse in different situations and for a longer period of time than you have. Their input is invaluable!

There are a number of websites that provide public information on criminal records, marital records, housing records, etc. Do your research. If you are not comfortable with what you discover, something is clearly not right. For additional information Google your state's case search (for the state of Maryland it would be; MDcasesearch.com).

Anger and Conflict

One aspect of your potential spouse's character you should be sure to examine is how they handle conflict. Specifically, you want to determine if they have been violent in any way or show signs that they are capable violence. If your potential spouse has ever been violent toward you, you should end the relationship immediately. If your potential spouse has threatened your life should you leave the relationship, seek legal protection immediately. Never enter into a covenant relationship with anyone who is abusive! God has something better in store for you!

Here are some questions you can use to determine if your potential spouse is a possible abuser:

- **Does he/she use harsh words to you or others?**

- **Do you feel that his/her tone or choice of words is disrespectful?**

- Does he/she ever talk down to you or offend you in anyway? (Look at how he/she speaks to other people — even the waiter at a restaurant — and TAKE NOTE!)

- Is your opinion valued and respected, or minimized and dismissed?

- Do you see signs of uncontrollable anger?

Based on your responses to the above questions, what is God leading you to do?

Christian Beliefs and Practices

II Corinthians 6:14 tells us not to be "unequally yoked," which means the two of you must be moving in the same direction towards Christ. Being "born again" is not enough. There are many people who confess to being "Christians" but are walking down a destructive path. They may have accepted Christ, but have not chosen the path of discipleship. If you actively attend church but your potential spouse only commits to going on "special days," then you are not moving in the same direction. If you believe in tithing but your potential spouse does not, you are not moving in the same direction.

Consider these questions:

- **What are your potential spouse's Christian beliefs?**

- **Are these beliefs consistent with yours? Can you say you and your potential spouse love God with all your heart, mind and soul?**

- What do you think the risk to your marriage would be if your potential spouse does not have a true love for God?

- List 3 of the worst things you can think of that can happen in your future marriage? Are you willing to stay committed "For Better or For Worse"?

- Make a list of your 3 most favorite activities. Make a list of your potential spouse's favorite activities. Indicate next to each activity if is pleasing to God. What conclusion can you draw from this exercise?

Alan and Jackie

Alan and Jackie were courting for one year. Alan was not committed to a local church, but Jackie was. Alan knew how important church was to Jackie. He knew he had to make a commitment to become a church member before

Jackie would move forward in marriage. He joined Jackie's church and became active in a ministry. However, shortly after marriage, Alan became disinterested in spiritual life and stopped attending church.

- **What do you believe happened in this scenario?**

- **How could this have been prevented?**

- **What signs did Jackie see prior to marriage?**

Honesty

Honesty is the key to removing the mask. You must be honest with yourself and your potential spouse. You need to take a really good look at how you feel about yourself in the relationship. It is important to be true to yourself and what you are feeling deep inside.

What you feel deep down is a true revealer—so don't minimize it.

Ask yourself the following questions:

- **Are you blossoming and growing spiritually in the relationship?**

- **Do you feel you are forcing things to happen?**

- **Are you more excited about moving forward than your potential spouse?**

- **Are you the one reading this book while he/she remain disinterested?**

- **Are you selfless? Is your potential spouse selfless? If not, what things do you both need to do to become more selfless?**

Remember, you and your potential spouse must adequately address these issues before marriage. Failure to address any one of them can result in marital discord and heartbreak. No marriage will be perfect, but the more work you do on the front end with respect to removing the mask, the more successful your marriage can be.

Discussion Questions:

- **In what way(s) do you and your potential spouse need to improve in each area addressed in this chapter (relationships, finances, background, anger, Christian beliefs, honesty)?**

- **What actions will you take to address these areas?**

- **Do you need to step back from the relationship to allow God to work on you or your potential spouse in any of these areas?**

As you work to remove the mask of your potential spouse, you must be willing to remove your own mask. Only then can you give and receive God's best!

Closing Prayer

Lord, I pray that You guide me as I discover the person I believe may be my mate. Help me to see things from Your perspective. Show me what I need to know to make the right decision. Help me to remove my mask. Help me to be honest with You, with myself, and with my potential spouse, that our relationship might honor You. If I choose to walk away, give me the grace to do so. If I choose to stay, let it be according to Your will.

Chapter IV:

So What Should You "Be"come Before Marriage?

Making the decision to marry is one of the most critical decisions you will ever make in your life. Therefore, it is important that you are adequately prepared for this lifetime journey. This chapter is designed to help you look at ten things you should strive to "Be" prior to marriage. If You Think You Want to Get Married, then developing yourself in the following key areas prior to making the commitment will ensure you are adequately equipped to select the proper mate. It will also make you a better spouse.

1. Be in Christ.

To be in Christ means to know and follow the teachings of Christ so you can be successful as you journey through marriage. As you consider marriage, strengthening your relationship with Christ will help you understand the plans and purposes God has for your life. It will also help you be open to hearing His voice (see Chapter I) so you can get His direction on the best life mate He has for you. Therefore, it is extremely important that you

> To be in Christ means to know and follow the teachings of Christ so you can be successful as you journey through marriage.

have a strong personal relationship with God through Jesus Christ. The first step in establishing that relationship is by repenting of your sins and accepting Jesus as your Lord and Savior

Romans 10:9-10 says, "if you confess with your mouth the Lord Jesus and believe in your hearts that God raised Jesus from the dead you will be saved."

Read the passage in your Bible and ask yourself the following questions.

- **Have you accepted Christ as your personal Lord and Savior?**

- **Do you really believe in Him with all your heart?**

- **Do you believe that Jesus not only wants to save your life but that He also wants to lead your life? Is He really Lord (owner) of your life?**

- **If you are already a believer, what additional things do you need to do to give God full control over your life?**

For God to truly lead your life and give you the direction you need, you must spend quality time with Him by praying and studying the Scriptures.

- **What are some ways you can improve your quality time with God?**

Psalm 119:11-16, 33-40 teaches us the importance of studying the Scriptures. Read the passages in their entirety and write down specifically what God is saying to you and how studying God's Word will benefit you.

2. Be Connected.

It is important to be connected to other Christians. Hebrews 10:24-26 teaches us to encourage each other to love and to do good towards one another. To always be willing to meet together. In doing this, you are in a better position to see where God is taking you. Others who are like-minded will support you in your journey through prayer and accountability.

- **Are you connected to other Christians in a local church?** *Read Hebrews 10:24-25.* **What is God saying to you in this passage?**

- **In what ministries or community activities are you involved? If you are not involved in any, explain why?**

- **Do you have a Christian friend, mentor or family member who will hold you accountable to God's Word?**

- Do you have someone to pray with on a regular basis?

- Even if you answered "yes" to each of these questions, there may be other areas where you can improve. If so, where and how can you improve your connections?

3. Be Goal-Oriented.

Goals are critical for giving you direction in life. Without goals you will live an aimless type of existence. It is important that you set measureable goals regularly and work toward them. As a single person, you should have appropriate goals based on how God has gifted you. Do not wait until marriage to accomplish what God has equipped you to accomplish now. Is it your goal to start a business, finish school, buy a home, or travel the world? Are you motivated enough to strive to reach those goals while you are still single?

Did you know that God has goals for you to accomplish before marriage? It's your job to discern what they are and to pursue them now, because once you are married, you will have your spouse's feelings and opinions to

> Goals are critical for giving you direction in life. Without goals you will live an aimless type of existence. Therefore it is important that you regularly set measureable goals and work towards them.

consider. That is not to say that you cannot pursue goals once you are married, but once you marry, you and your spouse will have to be of one mind about these future plans.

- **What do you aspire to do?**

- **What has God directed or called you to do?**

- **What are your top five life goals?**

- **Does your potential spouse's goals line up with your goals?**

Habakkuk 2:2-3 teaches us "to write our vision and make it plain, for it has an appointed time but we must wait for it". In other words, write clear goals and make them measureable.

Read the passage in total to gain further insight.

Johnny and Liza

Johnny and Liza were married for five years before Johnny expressed his deep desire to pursue a career in music. Johnny had a stable job making a solid income. To fulfill this desire, he asked Liza to, essentially, act as a single parent to their two daughters while he used the family's savings to pursue his music career in another state. Clearly, Johnny should have fulfilled this dream before marriage, because he now has a wife and two children who need him to be present.

4. Be Smart.

Being smart about the person you are planning to engage in relationship with requires you to be open and fully aware of his/her character and behavior. Unfortunately in many relationships, the potential spouses tend to ignore red flags for a variety of reasons. According to author Ron Deal, people in dating relationships tend to put on rose colored glasses and red flags look pink. Red flags are those areas of a potential spouse's character or circumstances that raise significant concern as it relates to their ability to be in a healthy marital relationship. Therefore it is important to examine any and all areas of concern before you commit to a relationship that could ultimately end in disaster.

> Red flags are those areas of a potential spouse's character or circumstances that raise significant concern as it relates to their ability to be in a healthy marital relationship.

Being smart also means developing a list of non-*negotiable* things you are not willing to compromise on. These are things that are unacceptable to you and that you should not tolerate.

- **Make a list of your beliefs and values.**

- **Based on your list of beliefs and values make a list of what you will not tolerate (these are called your non-negotiables).**

- **Make a list of the things you do not like about your potential spouse.**

- **Compare your dislikes to your values.**

- **Based on your responses to the above, how do you believe you should proceed?**

It is critical that you DO NOT COMPROMISE YOUR VALUES AND BELIEFS when deciding on your life long mate. If you have a non-negotiable, DO NOT NEGOTIATE! It's just not worth it.

5. Be Balanced.

Being balanced means you and your potential spouse are on the same page of life. You should not enter into a relationship with someone with whom you have very little in common. More importantly, with someone who does not agree with your values and beliefs. This is particularly true in terms of your Christian beliefs.

In Chapter 3 we discussed not being joined together with those who don't have the same belief system (unequally yoked). How can two truly become one when you do not have oneness in your beliefs?

- **In your own words, describe what "unequally yoked" means.**

> You should not enter into a relationship with someone with whom you have very little in common. More importantly, with someone who does not agree with your values and beliefs. This is particularly true in terms of your Christian beliefs.

So You THINK You Want To Get Married

- Give at least two examples of how being unequally yoked could impact a marital relationship.

- What are the things you would like to have in common with the person you desire to marry?

- Make a list of the differences between you and your potential spouse. Then make a list of the similarities. Compare and contrast the two lists.

- What is God showing you through the similarities and differences?

- Can you live with the differences?

6. Be Patient and Content.

Patience and Contentment are two critical virtues that are needed to be successful in marriage. The first test is determining if you are rushing into marriage because of your lack of contentment in your single state. Do not rush into marriage. Instead, learn to be satisfied while in your single status.

God has ordained this time in your life to allow you to seek and establish your life's purpose. If you are not able to be content as a single person, you will struggle with being content as a married person. Do not allow family, peers, or other self imposed pressures to push you into making a decision to marry prematurely. There is a right time for everything. *Ecclesiastes 3 teaches us "there is a time and season for everything under the sun."* We must be in sync with God's timing in order to experience God's greatest blessing. Embrace your singleness with excitement!

Philippians 4:6-11 says "do not be anxious for anything but through prayer take your concerns to God". Additionally, learn to be content in whatever state you find yourself. Marriage will bring various challenges that will require you to embrace contentment. If you learn how to be content while single you

> Patience and Contentment are two critical virtues that are needed to be successful in marriage.

> Do not allow family, peers, or other self imposed pressures to push you into making a decision to marry prematurely.

So You THINK You Want To Get Married

will be better prepared to handle those marital challenges.

- **Study this passage further and write specifically what God is saying to you in this passage.**

7. Be Wise.

Wisdom is having the ability to see through the eyes of God. Listen to the voice of God for how He is directing you in making a decision about marriage. Marriage should not be an emotional decision, but one that is made based on biblical principles. For example, the Bible teaches us in the book of Ephesians that the husband is the head of the wife. If you are the potential husband, you must be equipped to lead, and if you are the potential wife, you must submit and follow. Are you able to live with that?
Read Ephesians 5:22-33 concerning the order of the family.

- **What is God saying in this passage?**

- Are you willing to embrace God's view on this?

Also Read Ecclesiastes 7:19 which teaches you to allow wisdom to drive you towards true power in embracing your role in marriage.

8. Be Educated.

Education is necessary in equipping yourself for any upcoming endeavor. Marriage is one of the biggest endeavors you will face but people do not deem it necessary to educate themselves prior to getting married. Unfortunately, they allow their feelings to be their guide. Feelings change regularly. You must use a more reliable barometer to determine if marriage is right for you. Be intentional about your future marriage by taking classes, getting premarital counsel, reading books, and asking reliable married couples questions about marriage. Study God's Word on marriage so you fully understand what God expects of you in marriage. Without intentionally preparing for marriage, you are setting yourself up for failure.

> Feelings change regularly. You must use a more reliable barometer to determine if marriage is right for you.

II Timothy 2:15 teaches us to study.

- **What is God revealing to you in this passage about educating yourself on marriage?**

- **After reading the passage, describe how you can you be more diligent in studying the Scriptures on marriage?**

> It is also important for you to gain a solid understanding of your spiritual gifts and talents. Becoming educated on how God has gifted you gives you a clearer understanding of the type of spouse that may be more compatible with you.

It is also important for you to gain a solid understanding of your spiritual gifts and talents. Becoming educated on how God has gifted you gives you a clearer understanding of the type of spouse that may be more compatible with you. Once you become aware of your spiritual gifts, God will be able to show you the type of person that best complements you.

To begin understanding your spiritual gifts, visit www.gifttest.org and take an initial assessment to help determine your gifts.

Read I Corinthians 12 and answer the following questions:

- What have you learned about your Spiritual gifts?

- Do your gifts and talents conflict with the goals and desires of your potential spouse? If so, you should not move forward, because this difference can cause major challenges in a marriage. For example, if you learn that you have a gift to teach and you desire to reside in a foreign country to teach but your potential spouse has no desire to travel internationally then this could be a huge issue for marriage.

9. Be Healed.

Healing is necessary in order for people to operate in a healthy manner in marriage. Unfortunately, many people enter into marriage with unresolved issues due to abuse, hurt, and un-forgiveness. An alarming statistic, reported by the National Center for Victims of Crime, shows that over fifty percent of people have experienced a childhood history

> If you do not get the counsel you need to deal with your issues prior to marriage, they will resurface during marriage.

of inappropriate touching or forced sex. Your past hurts, if not dealt with, can have a direct impact on your future marriage. Therefore the impact of these issues must be dealt with to ensure a successful marriage.

If you know you have unhealed wounds, you should not be ashamed to seek the counseling you need. In order to be the mate your potential spouse needs, it is paramount that you get these issues resolved in your single state. Doing so will eliminate a number of issues you may face in marriage. If you do not get the counsel you need to deal with your issues prior to marriage, they will resurface during marriage and you and your mate will have to live with the pain that these unresolved traumatic experiences can cause.

The residual anger and hurt from traumatic experiences can result in resentment toward your spouse, lack of sexual intimacy, and lack of trust. All of which leads to an unhealthy and unhappy marital relationship.

Proverbs 11:14 teaches us that getting advice makes a sure victory. If you want to be victorious in overcoming your past hurts and pains, get counsel and begin getting it resolved.

- **Do you have issues that need to be resolved? If so, what are they?**

- How do you plan to resolve them?

- In what ways do you think these unresolved issues can impact your future marriage?

10. Be committed for a lifetime.

Commitment is the ability to dedicate yourself to something for an extended period of time. In the case of marriage, it is dedication for a lifetime. So, before entering marriage, you must evaluate your ability to commit. You should enter marriage with the mindset that divorce is not an option. Malachi 2:16 teaches that God hates divorce, and therefore the marital commitment is intended to last until death separates you. If you enter marriage thinking that you will get a divorce if it does not work, you are destined for failure!

Exercise: Interview at least two people who have been through a divorce. Ask them the following questions so you can determine how the divorce impacted their lives:

> Marriage is dedication for a life time. Before you enter marriage, you must evaluate your ability to commit.

- What was the pain like?

- What are their regrets?

- How difficult was it?

- What did they learn from it?

- What did you learn from this exercise?

What is the worst thing you think can happen in your marriage?

Luke 1:37 teaches us that with God nothing is impossible, which means He can restore anything. Begin to develop a plan for overcoming your worst case scenario.

For additional information on getting help in any of these areas visit our website at www.SkipandBeverly.com

A Final Word about Singleness

Marriage requires sacrifice. I Corinthians 7:32 says singles are free to be concerned about the things of the Lord and how to please Him. How exciting to be fully devoted to Christ! However, you must remember that when you get married, many of the luxuries of singleness will have to be sacrificed. God requires that you put your spouse first.

Exercise:

- **Make a list of what you love about being single.**

Philippians 4:11 teaches us that you should be content in the state that you are in. If you cannot find enough things you like about singleness, it is an indication of your lack of contentment. This means that you will likely be discontent in some area of your marriage.

- **After completing your list, ask yourself if you are willing to give those things up. Why or why not?**

Chapter V:

So What Should You Think About Sex?

Almost every TV show, newspaper article, or magazine advertisement has sexual undertones. Society has inundated us with the need and desire for sex, so much so, that we believe we must indulge ourselves no matter the cost. Interestingly, if a politician or a celebrity decides to indulge in sexual excursions they are relentlessly ridiculed. Society has a double standard but God's standards have never changed.

God requires singles to be sexually pure, both physically and emotionally, until marriage. Sexual purity means abstaining from all sexual activity until marriage. This includes pornography, masturbation, oral sex, excessive sexual thoughts and conversations. However, this can be extremely challenging when you have strong sexual desires. Add to that, popular consensus says that it is normal and perfectly acceptable to engage in pre-marital sex, pornography, as well as excessive sexual thoughts and conversations.

> God requires singles to be sexually pure, both physically and emotionally, until marriage. Sexual purity means abstaining from all sexual activity until marriage.

- **Read I Thessalonians 4:3-8 which teaches us to abstain from sexual immorality. Determine what areas in this passage relate to you.**

"When you engage in continual sexual sin your view of the person you are in relationship with becomes jaded".

God is clear that you should abstain from sexual immorality. It is not His desire for you to be led astray and distracted by your lusts and passions as an unmarried person. He desires for you to focus your attention on fulfilling the purpose He has for your life.

Unfortunately, sexual immorality causes people to miss their God-given purpose because their ungodly sexual desires have driven them completely off track. It causes spiritual blindness, dishonorable lifestyles, impure perspectives, the wrongful handling of one's potential spouse in the sight of God and minimizes the joys of sex in marriage. Below are detailed reasons why you should maintain sexual purity:

Reason One: To Avoid Spiritual Blindness

Spiritual blindness is the inability to see God's view on a matter. It is caused by continual sin in your life. When you engage in continual sexual sin, your view of the person you are in relationship with becomes jaded. Your ability to see character flaws is limited because your desire for sex overpowers it. You begin placing high value on the emotional intimacy verses the truth of who you are. Your values begin to fade and you become much more willing to compromise. This puts you in a position of defeat before you have a chance to fully process how or if you should move towards marriage.

So, how can you know if you have become spiritually blind?

Romans 1:21 teaches us how our thoughts can become darkened (spiritual blindness) due to our lust and lies. Reflect on this passage and ask yourself these questions:

- **Are you more focused on your sexual desires than you are on God's truth about remaining sexual pure until marriage?**

- **Do you feel discontent with your singleness?**

- **Have you been engaging in premarital sex?**

- **Have you been more willing to compromise some of your values and beliefs?**

If you answered yes to any of these questions, it may be a sign that you are suffering from spiritual blindness. Ask God to give you the grace to remove the sin from your life so you are able to clearly see the direction He has for your life.

Reason Two: To Be Purified for God's Purposes

A second reason singles are to remain sexually pure is to eliminate impure perspectives concerning the purpose God has for your life. God's plan for us is to embrace His ways by separating ourselves from the way society says we should be. Society says it is okay to have sex before marriage, but God says, "No." I Thessalonians 4:3 says we should abstain from premarital sex.

Sexual immorality is displeasing to Him because sex was designed for marriage. The consequences of violating this principle are serious and come with great repercussions, which impacts God's plan and purpose for our lives.

In I Corinthians 6:9-10. God tells us that if we "practice" things that are displeasing to Him, there are severe consequences.

Joe and Cynthia:

Joe and Cynthia were in a long time sexual relationship. Joe was tired of the relationship and decided to move on. Cynthia was devastated. She decided she was not going to accept Joe's decision to move on because she had invested too much in the relationship. As a result she stalked Joe for several months. Everywhere Joe turned, Cynthia was there. She appeared at his job, at the stores where he shopped and would stake out his home late at night. Cynthia also called him relentlessly and shared how she could not live without him. Joe felt trapped and burdened by his decision to be sexually involved with Cynthia for so long.

- **What are some other consequences you can think of that are caused by sexual sin?**

- **What do you think Joe could have done differently?**

- **Why do you think it was so difficult for Cynthia to move on?**

God has great plans for our lives and He does not want us to become trapped by sexual sin. Jeremiah 29:11 tells us that God knows the plans He has for us. He wants us to live a life that is pleasing to Him so we can receive His best!

- **What plan do you believe God has for your life?**

- **How might the plan God has for your life be affected by sexual sin particularly if you were in Joe and Cynthia's situation?**

- List one thing you can do to guard yourself from sexual sin?

Reason Three: To Avoid a Dishonorable Lifestyle

I Thessalonians 4:3-8 is a command from God to live a holy and honorable lifestyle. The key is maintaining sexual purity. God's desire for you is to control your sexual desires and live a lifestyle that honors Him.

According to Webster's Dictionary, "Honorable" means respected, privileged, outstanding, distinct, living with purity and integrity. To live in this manner requires you to fully devote your words and actions to God. Allow His principles to totally guide your life and guide you to your life mate. More importantly, we want to be holy and honorable in the sight of God.

> God's desire for you is to control your sexual desires and live a lifestyle that honors Him.

Skip and Beverly:

Prior to getting married, we abstained from sex. We made it a priority to honor God and ourselves. It was difficult but we knew our future was dependent upon our decision to follow God's principles no matter what our flesh desired. Mastering this principle together and prior to marriage, has also allowed us to become selfless in other areas of our lives, which was an unexpected outcome. And in case you didn't know, selflessness is one of the hottest commodities in marriage. To this day, we believe God has shown favor to us in so many areas of our lives because of our commitment to an honorable lifestyle.

- **Do you believe your words and actions in your premarital relationship are holy and honorable in the sight of God?**

- **What areas do you think you can improve in?**

> Engaging in sexual activity with your potential spouse does them a disservice because it causes them to sin against God.

- **List one thing you can start doing to have a more honorable lifestyle.**

Reason Four: To Help Prevent Your Potential Spouse from Committing Sin

Engaging in sexual activity with your potential spouse does them a disservice because it causes them to sin against God.

I Thessalonians 4:6 teaches us that it is unacceptable to engage in this manner. Romans 14:13 says let no one put a stumbling block in the way of someone who is trying to obey the Word of God. Therefore, you should also watch your sexual undertones (things you wear, say and do), which may cause your potential spouse to struggle. By causing your potential spouse to sin now is only contributing to how you will handle other sinful activity once married.

Al and Joanne:

Al and Joanne had sex regularly while dating. They both felt deeply that it was wrong but Al was unable to overcome his physical desire for sex prior to marriage so Joanne obliged. After marriage, Joanne didn't feel as obligated to engage in sex as she did prior to marriage so she constantly made excuses not to engage in sex with her new husband.

Al became very frustrated and angry. As a result they both found themselves in a sinful state. Joanne violated God's principle found in I Corinthians 7:3-4 which teaches that the wife should not withhold sex from her husband. Al violated James 1:20 which states that the anger of man does not produce the righteousness of God. He also violated I Peter 3:7 which states that he should have dwelled with understanding with his wife.

Al had to learn that his violation of his wife's purity prior to marriage led to her lack of sexual desire after marriage. If they had just obeyed this principle, the impact in their marriage could have been minimized.

- How might this passage apply to you?

- What can you do to ensure that you do not follow a similar path as Al and Joanne?

> In I Corinthians 6:9-10, God warns us that if we establish a lifestyle of sexual immorality, we will not inherit the kingdom of God.

Reason Five: To Avoid Consequences from God

Think about the unfortunate consequences of past sexual relationships: the pain in letting go, the anger, the stalking, the obsessions, the unwanted pregnancies, the abortions, the sexually transmitted diseases, and more. All these consequences are God's way of underscoring His desire for you to remain sexually pure. The most serious consequence of violating God's command in the area of sexuality is mentioned in I Corinthians 6:9-10. In this passage, God warns us that if we establish a **lifestyle** of sexual immorality, we will not inherit the kingdom of God. Ask yourself if it is really worth losing your place in His kingdom.

- What are some consequences you have experienced in past relationships due to sexual immorality?

- List 1-2 things you will do to avoid these consequences.

Reason Six: To Maximize the Enjoyment of Sex as a Married Couple

> Sex outside of marriage dishonors God, the marriage covenant, and the person whom you intend to marry.

In Hebrews 13:4, God teaches us that sex within marriage is clean, but those who engage in sex outside of marriage will be judged. God is clear in letting us know sex was designed strictly for marriage. Having sex prior to marriage complicates the marital relationship because it creates unrealistic sexual expectations. Additionally, sex outside of marriage dishonors God, the marriage covenant, and the person whom you intend to marry.

Joe and Sarah

Joe and Sarah were having sex at least five to six times a week prior to marriage. Once they married, the reality of life as a married couple crept in: handling bills, working long hours, and a new baby. The expectation of sexual activity had been unrealistically set because they violated God's command. They became very dissatisfied and frustrated with their sexual intimacy as a newly married couple. Not only were they struggling to meet an unrealistic expectation but sex had become a chore.

- **Do you think waiting until marriage to engage in sex would have given them more excitement in their marriage?**

- **Not considering what others do prior to marriage, do you think waiting until marriage would be more honorable?**

- **Would God be pleased with your answer?**

> Waiting until marriage to have sex helps you learn to fight sin together as you trust God to keep you pure.

Reason Seven: To Learn to Trust God as a Team

Waiting until marriage to have sex helps you learn to fight sin together as you trust God to keep you pure. The desire for sex is a very powerful force that requires constant prayer and self-control to manage. To overcome it, you must learn to fight the desire. This is accomplished by constantly reading scriptures, praying, and setting and discussing boundaries.

Fighting sexual sin requires that both people come together and agree that you are going to adhere to God's principles by standing against the temptation of sin. So, when other challenges occur in your marriage, you will have experience in facing challenges together. Also, the fear of infidelity diminishes and trust is established because you have proven that you can abstain when necessary. In this way, you are learning to fight sin as a team. Ecclesiastes 4:9 teaches that two are better than one. When the two of you come together against sin with God as your guide; God will reward you.

- **How might trusting God in this area help you in other areas where you may be struggling with sin?**

- **What things will you do to fight the desire to entertain sexual sin?**

How do I Practically Maintain Sexual Purity God's Way?

Maintaining sexual purity as a single person when you have no potential spouse to tempt you does not present as great of a challenge. But that commitment and resolve is tested when you are courting a potential spouse and you are sharing intimate parts of your inner self with them and the two of you are spending lots of time together (many times alone). The following suggestions will help you to practically maintain sexual purity God's way:

Renew Your Mind

It is important that you understand what your mind and heart perceives influences your actions (Mark 7:21). Over time, society has slowly skewed our thinking concerning what is acceptable for our lives and in this case how we should engage in intimate relationships. None of these views line up with God's way. For example, society says it's okay to live together before marriage— "to try it before you buy it." But God tells us to marry the person and to abstain from sex until you do.

Romans 12:1-2 teaches us not to embrace society's way of thinking but to transform our thinking. To transform your mind, you must identify scriptures that will encourage you to re-examine your values regarding sexual intimacy. For example, maybe you need to rethink what you watch on TV as well as the type of conversations you engage in.

To help in this area, read I Corinthians 7:32 to learn that prior to marriage, we should focus on how to please God, not how to please a person we are not yet married to. Remember the key is to be vigilant in keeping God's perspective in mind.

- **What areas do you think your mind needs to be renewed?**

- **If having a more solid understanding on sexual immorality is an area of concern visit www.biblegateway.com. Do a word search on sexual immorality and begin studying God's view on this issue. This approach applies to any area where you want to renew your mind.**

Lay Down Your Sexual Desire

God reserved sex for marriage. You have a responsibility to honor and please God by waiting until marriage before engaging in sex. Be willing to put aside your sexual desire **so you can honor God** and your potential spouse. As discussed in the previous sections of this chapter, doing this has significant benefits. However, not laying down your desires prior to marriage comes with significant consequences.

When Jesus laid down His life for us, He did it to save us from sin (John 3:16). Similarly, you can save yourself as well as your potential spouse from the sin of sexual immorality and the consequences associated with it.

Do not allow your own desires to tempt you to sin against God. God has a perfect gift called marriage for you, so do not tear the wrapping and tatter the box before it is time.

- **Read James 1:13-17. Write down what this passage is saying to you.**

Ask God for Grace

Grace is God's power to help you do what you cannot do in your own strength. He can give you the ability to control your sexual desires but we must be willing to ask Him. God knows that we have weak moments but He teaches us in II Corinthians 12:9 that His Grace is sufficient for us and His Power can work in us when we are weak. When you are weak and feel overcome by your sexual desires, God's grace can sustain you.

Get an Accountability Partner

Find a godly person who can hold you accountable in keeping God's Word. Ask your men's ministry or women's ministry at your church to recommend someone. You could also identify a co-worker, a family member, or someone whom you believe leads their life according to the Word of God. The purpose is to find someone that can help you live according to God's principles. Once you find that person, you have to commit to being open, listening and following the godly direction they may be giving you.

- **List specific ways that an accountability partner can help you? Proverbs 27:17 teaches us that we can improve each other.**

Exercise

The following exercise will help you to set the appropriate boundaries with your potential spouse so that you can avoid the traps caused by sexual desire.

Set Boundaries

a. Determine what your sexual temptations or triggers are and set boundaries that keep you from giving in to those triggers. Share your lists with your potential spouse.

b. After you develop a list of boundaries that address those triggers, create a consolidated list of boundaries that will help you maintain and protect sexual purity. For example, one person's boundary might be to abstain from heavy kissing but the potential spouse did not list it as a boundary. It should however, be added to the consolidated list and all boundaries should be honored.

Commit to a Purity Pledge

Once you and your potential spouse have committed yourselves to sexual purity, seal your commitment by developing and dedicating yourselves to a purity pledge. Use the sample pledge below or develop one that speaks to you specifically. It can be as short or as long as you like. Once you have developed the pledge, sign and keep it in a place of honor. Both potential spouses should write their own pledge and then there should be a "ceremony of exchange" which may also involve the exchange of a token or memento to serve as a reminder of the pledge.

Sample Purity Pledge

Father, I pledge to You to be sexually pure based on Your Word and to honor that commitment with my potential spouse until the day we are married.

Signature/Date

Chapter VI:

So What Should You Think About Roles in Marriage?

For any organization to succeed there must be order, and those involved in that organization must have specific roles. In many organizations, there are Presidents and Vice Presidents or Chief Executive Officers (CEOs) and Chief Operating Officers (COOs). What would it be like if there was no order, structure or specified roles in organizations? The company would be chaotic and disorganized. The same is true for marital relationships. Without structure or organization, the relationship will also be chaotic and disorganized.

Throughout Scripture, the role of husbands and wives is depicted as an essential function to the fruitful operation of a marital relationship. The role is indicative of each person's responsibility, not their importance. In Genesis 2, I Corinthians 7 and Ephesians 5, a man's role in marriage is described as being the head, protector and provider, while a woman's role is described as helper, submitter, and respecter.

In many marital relationships, roles can be viewed in one of three ways: traditional, non-traditional, or biblical. The traditional

> A man's role in marriage is described as being the head, protector and provider, while a woman's role is described as helper, submitter, and respecter.

marital relationship consists of the husband being the primary breadwinner with limited involvement in parenting the kids and with no household responsibilities. In this traditional marital role, the husband independently makes all decisions and thus devalues his wife. In Western culture, we saw this mostly in the 19th and 20th centuries.

Next are the non-traditional roles which came in the late 20th and 21st centuries. In a marriage with non-traditional roles, there are no defined responsibilities. Consequently, tasks in the marriage were accomplished according to who "felt" like addressing a need. Bills are frequently split 50/50, regardless of income. In this model, decisions are made based on who has the most expertise or money. In some cases, living together before marriage is considered a prerequisite and a method to test the relationship prior to getting married.

Finally, the biblical view which is God's perspective on the marital relationship. In Genesis 1:27, God created BOTH male and female in His own image. Then, Ephesians 5:23 tells us that the husband is the head of the wife as Christ is head of the Church. However, " head" does not imply that one is greater or better than the other. God makes that clear in Genesis 2:20b, when He says He created a helper for man who was comparable to him. "Helper" was never intended to be a derogatory term but is defined in this passage to mean a shield against the enemy. The word "comparable" means to be equal or just as important. So simply speaking, God has given spouses different roles but equal importance.

Therefore the roles described below are the biblical foundations upon which marriages are built.

Role of the Husband

In Luke 22:24-27, God says those who govern or lead should be servants. As leaders of the home, husbands are expected to be servant leaders. A servant leader is one who has the authority to be served but chooses to sacrifice for the sake of others. Ephesians 5:25 gives us a clearer picture; Husbands should love their wives as Christ loved the Church and sacrificed Himself for the Church. Husbands as servant leaders, should use as their model, the sacrificial love that Christ has shown.

> Husbands as servant leaders, should use as their model, the sacrificial love that Christ has shown.

Love your wife sacrificially. As the husband, you should be willing to sacrifice your time by considering your wife's needs above your own. You should also be willing to embrace the things she likes. I Peter 3:7 teaches us to dwell with understanding and give the wife honor. Honor her by joining her in her world. Embrace her likes, dislikes, hopes and dreams. Follow through on commitments you make to your wife. Compliment and praise her regularly.

Sacrificial love is being content with your wife by giving her your undivided attention and not being distracted by other women and other things (sports, job, etc.). It also requires that you encourage her to grow into being the woman God has called her to be. Finally, be willing to continually learn your wife by

> "Husbands, likewise, dwell with them with understanding, giving honor to the wife, as to the weaker vessel, and as being heirs together of the grace of life, that your prayers may not be hindered." I Peter 3:7

So You THINK You Want To Get Married 85

seeking counsel, reading resources to improve your relationship and by praying regularly.

Ask yourself the following questions:

- **Do you think you could love your wife sacrificially?**

- **If so, why? If not, what do you think your challenges will be?**

- **In what areas will you need support in loving sacrificially?**

Be a living example of what God teaches in His Word so your wife has a godly example to follow.

Sanctify and cleanse your wife with the Word of God. Be a living example of what God teaches in His Word so your wife has a godly example to follow, thereby being sanctified and cleansed. Be even-tempered by not allowing anger to control your responses to her. Practice self-restraint and self-control so your temper is not easily provoked. Be sober-minded and not extreme in your thinking and your conversation with her. Make sound

86 *So You THINK You Want To Get Married*

decisions that are based on Godly principles. Have good behavior so much so, that your reputation precedes you. You should have a reputation that makes you worthy to follow (See 1Timothy 3:1-2).
Ask yourself the following questions:

- **What do you think you will need to do to sanctify and cleanse yourself in the Word of God?**

- **How might this be a challenge for you?**

- **Give an example of how you would cleanse your future wife through God's Word.**

Present your wife blameless by covering her wrongs, hurts and pains. To present your wife blameless, you must be blameless so your wife and no one else can speak evil of you or about you. This role reminds me of a great book by authors Bob and Audrey

Meiser, *Marriage Under Cover*. This book reveals the true story of how Bob covered his wife, Audrey, when she became pregnant as a result of an adulterous relationship. By the grace of God, Bob was able to cover and forgive her and present her blameless before their family and friends.

Presenting your wife blameless requires you to be a protector by identifying any areas that may cause stress or pressure for the family. This requires you to depend on the grace of God as opposed to negative influences that can produce negative and sometimes devastating consequences. Always deal with issues head on by being up front and ready to confront truth in a sober manner. Be sure to have a small group of men who can hold you accountable–mentors and mentees.

Nourish and cherish your wife daily. Recognize her as a precious jewel that should be handled with care.

- **Read Proverbs 31:10 and write why you think this passage refers to a wife's value as greater than a ruby.**

I Peter 3 says wives are the weaker vessel, much like China. China is durable but breakable, so be careful with the arguments you have and the words that are spoken. Speak words that encourage and do not break your wife's spirit. Be kind and gentle with your wife. Be open to new ways of doing things and respond gently when she comes to you with a request. Include her in all decisions and ensure that her temporal needs are met. Taking this posture makes your wife feel valued.

Ask yourself the following questions:

- **Why do you think wives are more fragile than their husbands?**

- **What can you do in your current situation to prevent breaking your potential wife (like China)?**

Leave and Forsake others and cleave to your wife (Genesis 2:24). In the very beginning of creation God teaches us that once we are married, we must detach from our family. This means not allowing their input to control our new family dynamic. Your role is to provide safety and security in all areas without division and discontent. So, be willing to forsake friends who may cause strife and insecurity in your marriage. Remember, molding into oneness can only occur when outside factors do not interfere with the process.

Cleaving to your wife requires that you include your wife in your vision. You should work with her to set the moral tone and biblical direction for the family. Always be ready to embrace God's way of doing things by not allowing negative influences to derail you.

Ask yourself the following questions:

- **Are there people in your life you need to leave behind for the sake of having a marriage?**

- **Will that be difficult for you? Why or why not?**

- **Do you believe you can fulfill the roles of a husband?**

- **Where do you fall short?**

- Are you truly committed to the teachings of God, or do you prefer to do things your own way?

Final Encouragement to Potential Husbands

While stepping up to being a husband may be a tall order, with God all things are possible. When God gives you the direction to marry, He will also give you the grace you will need to be successful in your marriage. II Corinthians 2:9 teaches us that His grace is sufficient for you and His power is made perfect in your weakness. God can and will give you the grace to be a great husband but it starts with truly placing your trust in Him.

Role of the Wife

In Titus 2:1, we are introduced to Titus, a young pastor, who was assigned to set the church of Crete in order. The people of Crete were being deceived by false teachings and were morally relaxed. The same can be said of what is happening in today's society, especially in relationships. Couples have embraced the values practiced in today's society and have become morally relaxed as it relates to God's instructions on the roles in marriage.

Ephesians 5:33 says husbands should love their wives as they love themselves but wives should respect their husbands.

- **In Titus 2:4-6 and I Peter 3:1-6, God gives clear instructions as to the role of the wife. Read these passages and write in your own words what you believe God is saying concerning the role of the wife.**

Below are six key roles of the wife taken from Titus 2, Ephesians 5 and I Peter 3. Remember, these are roles that should be embraced after marriage, not before.

Respect your husband

Ephesians 5:33 says husbands should love their wives as they love themselves but wives should respect their husbands. According to Webster's Dictionary, respect means to give attention to, to hold in high regard, esteem, and refrain from interfering.
We have provided spiritual guidance and martial coaching to hundreds of couples and there is a significantly large percentage of men who feel disrespected by their wives.

- **Based on the aforementioned definition of respect, why do you think husbands feel so disrespected by their wives?**

There was a TV show a few years ago where the wife decided that she would help her husband get a job. She called an old boyfriend who owned a business and asked him to hire her husband. She asked the old boyfriend to make her husband believe he had gotten the job on his own merits. While she thought she was helping, she had actually interfered in the worst way, thereby disrespecting him. Her husband found out that she was behind it all and was extremely humiliated. This event created a huge wedge in their marriage which caused major distrust and betrayal.

- **What things can you do to avoid disrespecting your potential husband?**

Submission is defined as yielding to those in authority even when you think you are correct. It is allowing God to handle the situation through His authority, rather than handling it on your own.

Submit To Your Husband

According to Gothard's *Institute in Basic Life Principles*, submission is defined as yielding to those in authority even when you think you are correct. It is allowing God to

So You THINK You Want To Get Married 93

handle the situation through His authority, rather than handling it on your own.

Society has convinced women that submission is a bad word, likening it to being a door mat or a pushover. This has never been God's definition. Gothard goes on to say that God intends for us to submit for the purpose of protection; He wants us to be protected from things that are not our responsibility. Gothard uses an umbrella as an example by defining it as a protector from elements such as rain, heat, hail and the like. So it is in our marital relationship. Our husbands are the umbrellas of protection. God intends for us to get under their protection so *they* can be subjected to the elements of life. He designed them to handle it, not the wife. Unfortunately, many wives do not embrace this principle and begin taking charge of things that God intended for their husbands to handle. They soon find themselves stressed and overwhelmed and their husbands begin feeling disrespected.

Submission and faith go hand-in-hand. Submission requires you to yield to your husband and place your faith in God to handle any situation according to His will. This may not always look the way you would like it to look but you must trust that God has the situation in His complete control.

Proverbs 21:1 says "*the king's heart is in the hands of the Lord.*" Like the rivers of water, He can turn it whichever way He pleases. The word "king" in this passage represents authority. This Scripture is critical to understanding and embracing God's ability to reach into the heart and mind of the person in authority. When women submit, they allow those in authority to take responsibility for the things God intended them to handle. When wives refuse to submit, men are less likely to become the men God intended them to be. If men are not allowed to be the umbrella, they will never learn how to effectively protect their wives from the elements of life.

- **Read I Peter 3:1-6 and Ephesians 5:21-24. What do you believe God is saying about submission?**

Comfort your Husband

In Genesis 2:18a, we learn that God did not want man to be alone so He created woman for him. God specifically created woman to fill the void of loneliness in man.

Do not neglect your husband while you are engaging in other pursuits. Many women are making companies successful while their husbands are left alone to manage things that are a wife's responsibility.

Marriages are suffering. You must appropriately balance your priorities by making your home and the needs of your husband your first priority. What sense does it make to rise to the top of your company while your home life drops to the bottom of a pit? You should be willing to put more energy into your family than your career.

Therefore it is important that wives make their husbands' needs a priority. I Corinthians 7:34 tells us to focus on how we can please our husbands. Wives should make their husbands' needs a priority over everything else.

How would you make your future husband a priority?

Help your Husband

In Genesis 2:18b, God calls on wives to help, not hinder their husbands. As a wife, you become a helpmate to your husband. Your husband should be able to depend on you to help him in any area needed. Being a helpmate does not equate to being a gofer or a secretary. The word "helper" in Genesis 2:18 is the same word that God uses when He says He is our help in Psalm 121:1. In this passage, God is our shield and protector against the enemy. He is our protector in times of need, trouble, pain, discouragement or confusion. So it is with the role of the wife as helper.

Wives are called to protect their husbands by giving them loving feedback on potentially bad decisions. To protect them against schemes of ungodly men and women, and to allow them to share their deepest pain without judgment.

> Your husband should be able to depend on you to help him in any area needed.

Remember as helpmates, wives lovingly protect, but not at the expense of respect or submission.

Be a Homemaker

Titus 2:5 tells wives to be homemakers, which means to tend to the home. The home should be one of the wife's primary responsibilities. The virtuous wife in Proverbs 31 had many responsibilities and multiple jobs, but her home was her top priority. This does not mean that the household responsibilities cannot be divided, but ultimately, the home is the wife's responsibility.

- **Read Proverbs 31:10-31. What do you believe this passage is saying about being a homemaker?**

Be a Nurturer

A nurturer is someone who further develops, cares for and educates. Titus 2:4-5 tells wives to nurture by loving our children. To be sensible, pure, and good. To be sensible means to be wise in what we say, understanding of our husband's needs and be practical in our actions and spending. To be pure means to stop dwelling or focusing on the negative; instead, focus on positive attributes of your husband. Be pure and innocent in your actions, how you dress and how you represent your family. Lastly remember to be kind. Titus 2:5 tells us that, as wives, we should always be tender hearted and compassionate toward our husbands. Every man loves a gentle, kind and sweet woman!

- **Read I Peter 3:2-4. What do you believe God is saying about being pure?**

> The benefits of operating in your role as a wife are outlined in Titus 2:4-5. You give the home and marriage stability, which means your home operates more harmoniously and with less stress, confusion and frustration.

The benefits of operating in your role as a wife are outlined in Titus 2:4. You give the home and marriage stability, which means your home operates more harmoniously and with less stress, confusion and frustration. You can clearly see what God has called you to do. When you function properly in these roles, you are able to see the path God has laid before you and fulfill your life's purpose. You are able to enjoy the fruits of a harmonious home. This includes stable minded children and husbands who feel loved and respected. When we abandon these God-given roles, we dishonor God, not our husbands. It is God who has given these roles and responsibilities, not our husbands. Wives will have to answer to God for denying the role He has given.

This chapter on marital roles emphasizes that *everything* you do in your marriage should revolve around these roles. Unfortunately, our society has devalued the importance of these roles by claiming that they are not applicable for today, or that they are impossible to perform because wives now have careers to consider. Remember, the virtuous wife in Proverbs 31 took care of her home and had a career. She is our model wife. In Ephesians 5, Husbands are required to model Jesus as servant leaders. They should be willing to sacrificially love their families as Christ loves the Church.

If you expect to have a successful marriage these roles are not optional. Ask God to give you the grace to function in these roles if you believe He has a plan for you to marry.

Chapter VII:

So What Should I Expect?

Expectation is defined as the act or state of looking forward to, anticipating or having confidence that what is desired will happen. Marriage is filled with expectations. When you select a spouse, you are choosing a whole lot of other things that must be considered. Therefore it is imperative that expectations are thoroughly discussed. Spouses are expected to communicate in a certain way, handle finances in a certain way, know the other's sexual needs, and more. High expectations are placed on one another. As a result, expectations are not met and disappointment surfaces.

> Marriage is filled with expectations. When you select a spouse you are choosing a whole lot of other things that must be considered. Therefore it is imperative that expectations are thoroughly discussed.

Karl and Sonia

Karl and Sonia were newlyweds. They both stepped into marriage with expectations that had not been discussed but felt their expectations were understood. Karl thought Sonia would cook and clean daily and engage him in sexual activity at least three to four times a week. Sonia, on the other hand, thought Karl would engage her in conversation every evening when he came home. She also thought he would immediately take care of all the repairs needed around the house. Neither of them met the other's expectations and they both were quite frustrated with marriage and each other.

In a marital relationship, there are some expectations that are reasonable and should be discussed prior to marriage. The topics and thought provoking questions in the following section will give you a basis for properly setting expectations in order to minimize hurts and disappointments.

1) **Communication**

> "Let no corrupt word proceed out of your mouth, but what is good for necessary edification, that it may impart grace to the hearers."
> Ephesians 4:29

Communication is critical in marriage. How you communicate can make or break a marriage. Ephesians 4:29 tells us not to speak corrupt words but to only speak in ways that edify others. Therefore, couples must set proper expectations on how to communicate with each other because everyone has different communication styles and various pressure points.

- **Share with your potential spouse how you react when disagreements occur.**

- **Discuss your method of resolving conflict.**

2) **Finances**

    Matthew 6:21 says where your treasure is there your heart will be also. How a person handles finances reveals a great deal about his/her character. It is the character flaws related to financial management that is among the leading causes of divorce. Therefore, it is important to discuss expectations related to managing finances.

    > How a person handles their finances reveals a great deal about their character.

    - **List your financial values (i.e. tithing, percentage of savings). Discuss them with your potential spouse.**

    - **What will your financial challenges be and how will you resolve them?**

3) **Children**

    Psalm 127:3 tells us children are a blessing from God, but the process of agreeing on establishing a new family or blending a family can be stressful if expectations are not properly set. Here are a couple of things to consider:

- Do you both want kids? Why or why not?

- What are your core values with raising kids and do they align with your potential spouse's values?

4) **Ministry and Profession**
   Ministry responsibilities, careers, and educational aspirations play a significant role in marriage. They can be demanding and very draining on a marriage if not placed in proper perspective.

   - **Discuss your ministry and professional aspirations with your potential spouse**

- Are you both in agreement with each other's aspirations? What adjustments will need to be made?

> Sex was designed for marriage. I Corinthians 7 says you should freely give your bodies to one another.

5) **Sex, Sex, and More Sex...**
   Sex was designed for marriage and I Corinthians 7 says you should freely give your bodies to one another. Without a doubt sex is a very critical component in marriage. Where it falls on the priority list is important because the frequency can vary, based on you and/or your potential spouse's needs and desires.

   Realistic expectations should be set in this area and adjusted regularly based on the season of life your marriage is in (i.e. having a new baby may limit the amount of sexual activity for a period of time).

   - **How often do you require sex?**

   - **How might this expectation differ from your potential spouses'?**

So You THINK You Want To Get Married 105

6) **Daily Life**
Setting the proper expectations about how you will lead your daily lives is a must! Simple decisions can become a serious point of contention. You must realize that dating is very different than marriage so you cannot expect the same day to day interaction. Here are some questions to consider:

- How will you engage with each other's friends and family on a regular basis?

- How will the home be managed (house cleaning, lawn work, etc...)?

> It is imperative that you and your potential spouse are equally yoked. This means that you both are traveling in the same direction as it relates to your Christian beliefs and practices.

7) **Christian Beliefs and Practices**
It is imperative that you and your potential spouse are equally yoked. This means that you both are traveling in the same direction as it relates to your Christian beliefs and practices. Your marital relationship will suffer extreme difficulties if your Christian belief systems are not the same.

Allison and George

Allison was very committed to her Christian beliefs. She worked diligently in the hospitality ministry in her church and attended Bible study weekly. George, however, had a lackluster commitment to Christ. He didn't think ministry involvement was necessary, therefore he only attended church twice a month on Sundays when time permitted.

After marriage, George stopped attending church all together. Allison was frustrated because George had very little godly guidance to offer to their family. He also shared that he really didn't think the Bible was the only guiding truth. Clearly, Allison and George had a major disconnect in a very critical component of their life together which drew a huge wedge in their marital relationship.

- **What Christian Values do you have that you will not compromise?**

- **How will you ensure that you don't end up like Allison or George?**

Setting Reasonable Expectations

As stated at the beginning of this chapter, no one will be able to live up to each and every one of our expectations; however, there are some things that you should not compromise on. For example, if your potential spouse is really clear that he or she does not desire children, and you are clear that you do, you need to continue your search for someone who shares that desire. In other areas, you will simply have to agree to disagree. Finally, any expectations held by you or your spouse must be reasonable and clearly stated.

Understand Who You Are Marrying

Your expectations of your potential spouse must first and foremost take into account how God wired them. Expectations are only reasonable if they are doable based on your potential spouse's capabilities.

What you should know in order for you and your spouse to set reasonable expectations:

1) Know your potential spouse's skills and gifts. Do not expect them to do something they are not gifted or capable of doing. For example, if she is not Henrietta House Keeper and He is not Harry Handyman, manage your expectations accordingly. You should agree to operate in the areas you are gifted to handle or develop alternatives, rather than expect each other to do something that neither one of you is skilled to do.

2) Know your potential spouse's love language. Gary Chapman, author of ***The Five Love Languages***, writes that each person has one of five primary ways they feel loved. They are receiving gifts, spending quality time, physical touch, acts of service, or words of affirmation. If you constantly give gifts to a spouse whose love language is spending quality time, you will never meet their "love" expectations. Please read the book to learn more about you and your potential spouse's love language. Understanding each other's love language will be critical in setting the right expectations.

3) Know your potential spouse's temperament. Their temperament and personality type determine how they respond and react to life's situations. Tim LaHaye's book, ***Spirit-Controlled Temperament***, provides insight in the area of temperament. LaHaye asserts that there are four primary temperament types; Choleric (Take Charge), Melancholy (Perfectionist), Phlegmatic (Peacemaker), and Sanguine (Fun loving). Understanding your potential spouse's temperament type will give you significant insight on why your potential spouse responds the way they do.

Geraldine and Larry

Geraldine and Larry had been married for five years. Geraldine was becoming very frustrated with her husband's slow response to major decisions that needed to be addressed in their home. She thought she had married a complete idiot. In reality, he just had a very different approach to handling things than she did. But she thought her approach was the right approach. After reading the principles in LaHaye's book, she began to understand her husband's temperament type and realized that he had a different approach to making decisions and she needed to be more understanding of the way God designed him.

Unfulfilled expectations and disappointments are inevitable in all relationships. The key is going to be how you set, discuss and manage your expectations so you are able to minimize future frustrations.

For more insight on how managing your expectations can reduce the negative impact on your future marriage, visit our website at www.skipandbeverly.com

Chapter VIII:

So What Should I Think about Parental Guidance?

P arental blessing is a vital component to a successful marriage. It is full and complete approval that parents are in agreement with supporting your decision to marry the person you desire. It is a signal that you have reached independence and are able to be 100 percent committed to your spouse in marriage. It is also a signal to you that your parents are fully committed to actively supporting the marriage.

When you marry, you are essentially marrying the entire family of your spouse, which means you allow them into your life. You are agreeing to deal with their challenges and family nuances. Therefore, without full agreement from the parents, the marriage can be strained.

God gave us parents to nurture us, develop us and give us life direction. He designed them specifically for us. We did not choose our parents and yet God commands us to honor them. See Ephesians 6. Throughout the Bible, particularly in the Old Testament, there are countless examples of how God used parents to give blessings to their children See Isaac's

> When you marry, you are essentially marrying the entire family of your spouse, which means you allow them into your life. You are agreeing to deal with their challenges and family nuances.

blessing in Genesis 27 & 28:1-4 and Jacob's blessing of his sons in Genesis 49. These passages show that God gives His stamp of approval through parents. In addition, men were required to "earn" their wives before fathers were willing to give their daughters in marriage. We believe this was a test of the male's commitment, diligence and faithfulness. See Jacob and Rachel's story in Genesis 29. Likewise, this parental blessing section will allow the parents to test their potential spouses' commitment as well.

Proverbs 21:1 teaches us that God ultimately directs the decisions of those in authority over us. Parents give a blessing, but other relatives/close friends can also give Godly counsel. While Godly counsel is good and is necessary when parents are no longer alive, it never overrides a parental blessing.

Who knows better than your parents and the people who have helped shape you what is best for you? Their guidance is essential in giving you advice needed to make a critical decision such as marriage. God has the hearts of your parents and those in authority over you in His hands. After all, He selected your parents for you, so ultimately, he is directing them to direct you. Isn't that wonderful!!! Therefore it is your responsibility to honor them by accepting the direction they are giving you.

Read Ephesians 6:1-3. Allowing your parents to give you a blessing tells them that you are giving them honor and respect. Incidentally, parents do not have to be born again believers to give you a parental blessing. Romans 13:1-2 teaches us that all authority is from God. Remember, we didn't select our parents, God did!

If you have a strained relationship with your parents perhaps this is your opportunity to bridge the gap.

For more information on parental guidance, please visit our website at www.skipandbeverly.com

Conclusion:

Remember, a dating relationship is very different from a marital relationship. The qualities that are most attractive in a dating relationship DO NOT work in a marriage: *he is fun, she looks great, we like going to the same places*, and so on. We are not saying these things are not important, but they are not the primary measures you should use to determine if a person is your future spouse. We use the analogy that dating couples are like fans at a ball game: enjoying watching the game, eating popcorn, cheering for their team, laughing, and hanging out with friends. The reality is that you are not participating in this game.

The game of marriage is very different from being in the stands. Once you enter the game, you must learn the plays in the playbook called the Bible. You must listen to the coach who is Jesus Christ. Take some hits, recover the ball and work hard to run touch downs. Always be willing to bounce back from fumbles and interceptions. Dating and marriage are totally different, so do not use the fun barometer of dating as a decision for marriage.

Ephesians 5 teaches us that marriage is the only earthly institution that represents Christ's marriage to the Church. Therefore it is important to God and must be taken seriously. God designed marriage for a man and

> Marriage is the only earthly institution that represents Christ's marriage to the Church. Therefore it is important to God and must be taken seriously.

a woman to create a miraculous union of oneness through Him. This oneness is achieved by avoiding any outside distractions that may interfere with the marital covenant. A marital covenant is an everlasting binding commitment established by God that cannot be broken. It is between a man, woman, and God, who commit to being together until death.

Just as you prepare yourself for your bride or groom on the wedding day you should prepare yourself to also meet God at the altar. Be ready to commit to Him fully by trusting and obeying Him to give you the grace to honor the marital commitment.